CELEBRATING THE CITY OF PHUKET

Celebrating the City of Phuket

Walter the Educator

Silent King Books

SILENT KING BOOKS

SKB

Copyright © 2024 by Walter the Educator

All rights reserved. No part of this book may be reproduced in any manner whatsoever without written permission except in the case of brief quotations embodied in critical articles and reviews.

First Printing, 2024

Disclaimer
This book is a literary work; the story is not about specific persons, locations, situations, and/or circumstances unless mentioned in a historical context. Any resemblance to real persons, locations, situations, and/or circumstances is coincidental. This book is for entertainment and informational purposes only. The author and publisher offer this information without warranties expressed or implied. No matter the grounds, neither the author nor the publisher will be accountable for any losses, injuries, or other damages caused by the reader's use of this book. The use of this book acknowledges an understanding and acceptance of this disclaimer.

Celebrating the City of Phuket is a collectible souvenir book that belongs to the Celebrating Cities Book Series by Walter the Educator. Collect them all and more books at WaltertheEducator.com

PHUKET

In Phuket's embrace, where the azure waves dance,

Celebrating the City of
Phuket

The symphony of the sea crafts a timeless romance.

Celebrating the City of
Phuket

Beneath the golden sun, where palm shadows play,

Celebrating the City of Phuket

Lies a paradise, where dreams gently sway.

Celebrating the City of
Phuket

On Patong's lively shore, where laughter meets the night,

Celebrating the City of
Phuket

Neon lights shimmer, a kaleidoscope of light.

Celebrating the City of
Phuket

Bars and markets hum with a vibrant beat,

Celebrating the City of
Phuket

In this haven of joy, life feels complete.

Celebrating the City of
Phuket

Through Old Town's alleys, a history unfolds,

Celebrating the City of
Phuket

With colorful murals and tales untold.

Celebrating the City of
Phuket

Mansions of yesteryears, rich with grandeur,

Celebrating the City of
Phuket

Whisper secrets of times, both pure and pure.

Celebrating the City of
Phuket

Temples of serenity, Wat Chalong stands tall,

Celebrating the City of
Phuket

A beacon of peace, inviting all.

Celebrating the City of
Phuket

With gilded spires and a tranquil grace,

Celebrating the City of
Phuket

Here, the spirit finds its sacred space.

Celebrating the City of
Phuket

Phuket's jungles, lush and green,

Celebrating the City of
Phuket

Cradle secrets unseen.

Celebrating the City of
Phuket

Waterfalls cascade with a melodic rush,

Celebrating the City of Phuket

Nature's chorus, in a harmonious hush.

Celebrating the City of
Phuket

From Kata's serene shores, where surfers glide,

Celebrating the City of Phuket

To Nai Harn's coves, where the tides reside,

Celebrating the City of Phuket

Phuket's beaches, a siren's call,

Celebrating the City of
Phuket

Breathtaking vistas enthrall.

Celebrating the City of
Phuket

In markets bustling, where aromas swirl,

Celebrating the City of Phuket

Thai spices dance, making senses twirl.

Celebrating the City of Phuket

Seafood fresh from the Andaman's embrace,

Celebrating the City of
Phuket

Every bite, a journey to a new place.

Celebrating the City of
Phuket

Big Buddha atop Nakkerd Hill, a sentinel so grand,

Celebrating the City of Phuket

Watching over Phuket, guarding the land.

Celebrating the City of
Phuket

A symbol of faith, compassion's pure light,

Celebrating the City of
Phuket

Guiding hearts through day and night.

Celebrating the City of
Phuket

Festivals bloom in riotous delight,

Celebrating the City of Phuket

Songkran's waters cleanse in playful fight.

Celebrating the City of
Phuket

Loy Krathong's lanterns float to the sky,

Celebrating the City of Phuket

Phuket's spirit soaring high.

Celebrating the City of
Phuket

In Phuket's embrace, every soul finds rest,

Celebrating the City of Phuket

A treasure of the Andaman, truly blessed.

Celebrating the City of
Phuket

A poem of life, in verses and rhyme,

Celebrating the City of
Phuket

Phuket, a paradise, transcending time.

Celebrating the City of
Phuket

ABOUT THE CREATOR

Walter the Educator is one of the pseudonyms for Walter Anderson. Formally educated in Chemistry, Business, and Education, he is an educator, an author, a diverse entrepreneur, and he is the son of a disabled war veteran. "Walter the Educator" shares his time between educating and creating. He holds interests and owns several creative projects that entertain, enlighten, enhance, and educate, hoping to inspire and motivate you.

Follow, find new works, and stay up to date with Walter the Educator™
at WaltertheEducator.com

Milton Keynes UK
Ingram Content Group UK Ltd.
UKHW020742110724
445512UK00011B/265